Feel the Fear but Start Your Business Anyway!

"10 Common Fears and How To Overcome Them"

By

Boomy Tokan

Copyright © Boomy Tokan 2013

All rights reserved. No part of this publication may be reproduced in any form, electronic or mechanical, including scanning, photocopying or any information storage or retrieval system without the prior written permission of the copyright holder.

Disclaimer

License Terms

This course is for your own personal use ONLY. It is STRICTLY PROHIBITED to reproduce the content enclosed herein or to distribute this course to any third party, or via any third party website. All content is protected by Copyright ©.

Income Disclaimer

This document contains business strategies, marketing methods and other business advice that, regardless of my own results and experience, may not produce the same results (or any results) for you.

I make absolutely no guarantee, expressed or implied that by following the advice below you will make any money or improve current profits, as there are several factors and variables that come into play regarding any given business.

Primarily, results will depend on the nature of the product or business model, the conditions of the marketplace, the experience of the individual, the application of said principles, and situations and elements that are beyond your control.

As with any business endeavor, you assume all risk related to investment and money based on your own discretion and at your own potential expense.

Liability Disclaimer

By reading this document, you assume all risks associated with using the advice given below, with a full understanding that you, solely, are responsible for anything that may occur as a result of putting this information into action in any way, and regardless of your interpretation of the advice.

You further agree that the author cannot be held responsible in any way for the success or failure of your business as a result of the information presented below.

It is your responsibility to conduct your own due diligence regarding the safe and successful operation of your business if you intend to apply any of this information in any way to your business operations.
COPYRIGHT © 2014 Boomy Tokan - ALL RIGHTS RESERVED.

FREE Bonus

How To Start Your Own Business In 30 Days"

Hey ... If you would like to learn how to start and run a "High Performance" business; then download this FREE guide. It will also show you how to start making money from your business within 30 Days!

<u>"How To Start Your Own Business In 30 Days"</u>

Copy and paste in your browser:
www.startyourownbusinessacademy.com/freedownload1

Enjoy

Content

Disclaimer

FREE Bonus

Introduction:

#1 Fear Of Failure

#2 Fear of Not Having Enough Money

#3 The Fear of Loneliness:

#4 "Fear of Fear of Losing Money"

#5 Fear of The Current Economic Conditions

#6 Fear of Being Too Old To Start a Business Now!

#7 The Fear of Not Knowing Enough!

#8 Fear of Competition

#9 Fear of Taking Risks

#10 Fear of What People Have Said

Conclusion

FREE Bonus

Other Books by Boomy Tokan

"How To Write Your First Business Plan"

Introduction & Chapter 1

Book Title: Business Funding Secrets:

Read Introduction & Chapter 1

"70 Public Speaking Tips"

Read Introduction & Chapter 1

The Bad Girls Of The Bible

Read Introduction & Chapter 1

Profile

Introduction:

A few months ago I received this email from a client:

"Hi Boomy

I have not made much headway with my business idea. I am too afraid to not make money....
I am teaching right now. I hate it but it's better than no job."

Then it suddenly hit me that the reason why some of my clients and others with good business ideas refuse to start their own business is due to some kind of fear that has incapacitated them!

It was like having an "Aha"! moment. I realised the cause of some people continually coming to the same course and asking the same questions yet moving no further is the fear of starting.

A little bit of online research showed that 1000's of people are in this category. What is shocking is that I have heard so many awesome business ideas that I know would work well if the entrepreneur were committed to the venture. Yet such ideas remain what it is; an idea until someone has a similar thought from another place, another time and then put it to work.

Remember *"Cemeteries are full of unfulfilled dreams... countless echoes of 'could have' and 'should have'... countless books unwritten... countless songs unsung... I want to live my life in such a way that when my body is laid to rest, it will be a well needed rest from a life well lived, a song well sung, a book well written, opportunities well explored, and a love well expressed."*— Steve Maraboli

Hence the reason I am writing this book to help those who have been incapacitated by fear, unbelief and lack of forthright action. My goal is fourfold:

1. To make you understand that the thoughts of failure that go through your mind can be channelled into the springboard that enables success
2. Make you realise that some of the fear and doubt are natural companions to 100's of successful business owners. They have refused to let those thoughts stop them and so can you!

3. Provide the tools that enable transformation from fear to action in the shortest possible time

4. To give you the confidence needed to start your business journey

Each chapter is written to identify the problem, provide solutions and action steps that will enable progress.

Thomas Jefferson says *"Do you want to know who you are? Don't ask. Act! Action will delineate and define you."*

We must realise it is the lack of action – failing to act - that makes someone a failure. You never fail when you try – you learn lessons that will help your future. In actual fact those who start successful businesses are not smarter then you but your inaction is the sure way to failure.

It is my hope that the love and desire you have for starting and owning a successful business will drive out the fear that has held you and many others bound.

This book is dedicated to those that will take action.

Enjoy!

Boomy Tokan

#1 Fear Of Failure

When I was growing up there was always one person that the bullies never picked on in the playground. Not because he was the strongest or the most accomplished fighter but because he was the guy that never gave up.

So, even when he was defeated in one fight he was known to start another fight with the same person 5 hours later in a different location. This boy was known to have fought the same person 5-8 times until the strong caved in and begged him to stop. He won the war not because he was good but because he was tenacious. Even boys much stronger begged him to leave them alone and never fought with him.

That is the way we should approach having a successful business. The industry must come to realise that you will never give up or cave in and that every failure will spur you on to try harder. When that kind of winning spirit is established the earth will yield to anyone the success he/she deserves!

Top of the list of most common hindrances to starting a business is the fear of failure!

Sometimes this fear is disguised by logical excuses like:

"I am waiting for an upturn in the economy";

"I will start in the summer; I hear the winter months are not a great time to start a business"

"I am just waiting until I feel it is the right time"

"I will start but there are just too many things going on right now"

"When the children grow up then we can take such a risk"

The above list is not exhaustive. The real issue is that such people are afraid the business may fail and they could lose money or worst still; what would people say!?

Someone put it this way; nobody likes failure because likes fertilizers they stink but when applied corrected is the key to making the soil geminate and produce the best possible crops.

One of the major differences between those starting their businesses and those who are still waiting and hoping it will happen one day is that starters have learnt to manage the fear that accompanies every start up stage. It is interesting to note that whether it is starting for the first time, launching a new product or starting a new marketing campaign, fear is always present like a faithful brother! So in reality no matter what stage of the business process you are; some sort of fear will be there to accompany you. The real question therefore is not whether you feel the fear but the real issue is how you use that fear as a spring board to success.

So here are a few nuggets to bear in mind:

1. **Failure will help you succeed**. To explain what I mean, I want to borrow a popular quote by Jack Canfield it says "Everything you want is on the other side of fear." - Jack Canfield. The reality of the matter is this - Unless you fail, your chances of success are extremely limited. Bill Gates says that, success is a lousy teacher! That is so true because companies like Kodak and Swiss Watches teach us how quickly a business can lose their winning edge if they lack the much need innovation and product releases. This also goes for the individual who is playing it safe by staying in a job they know is not their burning desire. In the

end they would have wasted valuable time that could have been applied into a much more fulfilling life of starting their own business

2. **Failure will help you stay alert**. I always consider the usefulness of having the possibility of failing as the real impetuous to make success happen quicker. When there is a tendency to fail or not fully achieve an objective you become more alert and focused. This mindset can be applied into running your business venture too. Rather than be paralysed with fear turn that negative energy into a positive momentum for progress. You do that by being alert, carrying out the necessary tasks and reducing the risks through appropriate research.

3. **Failure is the way of removing the dust and exposing the diamond in you.** What is interesting is that unless you fail in some sense all the bad/wrong/obsolete ideas will still remain in your head and you still think they will work in the manner you envisage them simply because you have

not exposed them to the realities of the true market.

"If you don't try at anything, you can't fail... it takes back bone to lead the life you want" - Richard Yates

It is true that many would be business start ups have great ideas and I think some of those ideas will change our way of life but also there are methods conceived in people's minds that will not work. The way to get rid of those or modify them into a workable successful system is by using them. Those who fail to use them would not realise they are harbouring unworkable ideas. Also they limit the chance of getting the good ideas if they fail by not practicing - getting out there and making it work.

4. **Failure teaches you how to win.**
Many who know of one of the greatest boxers that ever lived – Mohamed Ali – love him because of his flamboyance, confidence, good looks and eloquent speeches. But equally to be admired was his tenacity to bounce back after defeat. As Trump has said: "Sometimes by

losing a battle, you find a new way to win the war."

How Do You Ensure Fear of Failure Never Keeps You from Starting In Business?

1. **Fear is normal:** one of the strongest negative thoughts that go around people's heads is that "If you are afraid to start it is because you are no good in business because the real business people are never afraid" That statement is utter nonsense!
   I cannot imagine anyone in business not having some element of fear or anxiety in the beginning and at strategic points. The difference is that, whatever challenge the seasoned entrepreneur has, he/she knows that there must be a solution lurking in the corner somewhere and so are automatically able to manage the effects of the fear!
   Understanding that fear is normal puts you in the category of the success and not that of the failures.
   Simply put – You Are Not A Failure You Are A Success – if you manage the fear that comes to your mind!

2. **Analyse what you are afraid of; and why you are afraid:** Sometimes people fear because we they lack understanding of the exact steps to take to establish the business or fear of quitting a job and committing fully to the process of starting a new venture. Maybe some are fearful because their friend or an associate started a business that recently failed. Whatever the fear it must be fully analysed.

3. **Work out steps that will mitigate the fear:** Once you have carefully analysed the source of the fear the next step is to determine how to mitigate that fear by setting up appropriate actions to bring it under control, reduce its negative effect and even convert/redirect it into positive energy.

    Let's take some examples from #2

    If we assume someone is fearful because they had a trusted friend whose business recently failed; what should be done.

    One useful solution is to find out what caused that particular failure; what the person learnt from it and what you will do if the pattern occurred within your own business.

Such understanding is immensely powerful and capable of providing the enlightenment necessary to transform fear to a positive/useful energy!

4. **Just start with "Baby Steps":** I once heard a statement by the famous motivation speaker Brian Tracy who asked "How do you eat an elephant?" he answered himself saying "one small piece at a time" We can relate that to a business and ask 'How do you start a High Performance business? By doing it one small piece at a time. Refuse to allow yourself to get swamped with the enormity of the set up tasks (see the chapter on the subject).
.
When you need to write a business plan slice it down to small bits. Think of what to research first, spread the work over weeks and months. Start small take baby steps and you will overcome the fear of starting.

Action Steps:

1. Get a pen and paper. Find a quiet place to think.
2. Write down all the aspects of starting a business that produces fear
3. Write down worst case scenarios if your business should fail.
4. Write down what you will do to mitigate them or solutions if they do happen.
5. Are you getting a clearer picture? Most of what you think will never happen and the ones that do happen; you will have a solution for it.

#2 Fear of Not Having Enough Money
In my experience there are always two extreme groups of those who are thinking about funding for their businesses. The first group are those whose business will need an enormous amount of money before they can start tit (that is what they think). The second group are those who do not need money to start a business yet believe they need an enormous amount of money.

Compound this with the thought of acquiring more debt and many people are incapacitated rather than start their dream businesses.

Whilst it is true that not having enough money can have serious negative reparations on the business, those who have too much money can suffer the same fate. For example; I know someone who spent about $90,000 on a music business project and had only sold about 10 CD's! That was a case of too much money causing stupidity.

However the fear that relates to funding is as real as you are reading this book so I am not going to belittle the emotion.

The real question therefore is not whether you feel the fear; but how you can use that fear as a spring board to success.

There are two questions you must ask about the subject of money:

1. **Is it more money you need or creativity?** When people are considering starting a business the tendency is to accrue unnecessary costs like; office, shop front; sales staff on salary etc. In fact, many have no idea of "Boots Strapping". The generally incorrect advice is that the small business must have at least 6monthsto a year's expenses saved before starting a business. How many people have that kind of savings I ask?
In reality most people can just about pay their current bills; that is why they want to start a business and not stay on the bread line!
The owners of The Grocery Game; Teri Gault who appeared on Good Morning America and in the book <u>**The Turnaround: Extraordinary Stories of How Ordinary People Turned Their Dreams**</u> tells us how she turned less than $100 into a business that now

grosses more than $1million turnover. If that does not impress you then the story of **Nebraska Furniture Mart** will definitely turn on your juices. She started the business with $500 investment and now it occupies 77 acres and currently owned by Berkshire Hathaway; Warren Buffet's company – you know he paid millions for it!

In the two businesses mentioned above; what set them apart was not the size of loans or major investments but the creativity and market positioning. There is a tendency among start-up businesses to throw money at challenges that require well thought out ideas - be careful!

What I continually find interesting is that most people who want funding (at least 80%) do not actually need it. What they need restructuring. Of the other 20% 15% of them can do the business with less money than they are asking for and only 5% actually have their financial needs on the button.

Essentially - creativity wins the race.

You have creativity! Whether you know it or not, I want you to realise that you have an immense amount of creativity. What I mean is that anyone who can think up a business project and can conceive of actualizing their plan must be able to create enough to overcome the initial financial challenge. Most people need not get into debt.

What I am going to do now is to give you 4 ideas you can use to side step the need for start-up capital. These ideas will help you alleviate money worries and the fear it posses that stops people from actually starting their own businesses. I am aware that a few people need investments but your first port of call must be to explore the 4 ideas outlined below:

1. **Get paid first:** Sometimes it is very possible to get the clients to pay you first and then use their money to create the products you sell to them. Obviously there are some risks involved like what happens if the process does not go according to plan and you end up owing your clients money or they want a refund! These are some of the realities of

running a business but getting your clients to pay upfront can dramatically make you cash rich overnight.

I remember a time we used to source properties for investors; they gave us a deposit of $2000 before we agreed to find them properties. What that deposit achieved was to eliminate the unserious clients and also provide us with good cashflow. Thank GOD it all went well. The more defined your niche and the bigger the problems you solve the more likely people will pay upfront. Can this apply to your business?

2. **Suppliers repayment terms:** Another great method of eliminating the need for money is to ask your suppliers for a long repayment period coupled with a duration that allows you to collect money from your clients before you have to pay the supplier.

Again I know this can help some businesses more than others. Imagine you supply furniture to individuals who pay you 7 days before delivery but you pay your suppliers every 30 days. This gives you enough time to even earn interest on the money; invest in shares (if you know what you are doing) before you pay your supplier.

3. **Use your savings:** It amazes me that whenever people talk about a bank loan or any other kind of funding they speak as though the money is free and cheap. Let me clarify; money is expensive to borrow.
Therefore cut your business actions to a size you can initially afford.
Using your savings for a well thought out plan must be your priority
so that whatever happens you can always have a second, third, fourth etc opportunity to restart if necessary.

4. **Find a friendly uncle with money:** Family members can be a great source of cheap loans but be careful not to do business with members who are fearful of taking risks.
If you have a good friendly uncle with money to throw around; the chances are he will give you cheaper loans than any bank. If he understands business and loves you at the same time then your financial worries are over.

Make sure you have your agreement on paper so that money does not ruin your relationship for ever. My book on Raising Funding gives you practical tips on the subject.

In conclusion be reminded that it is not having enough money in bank that creates the success you want but having a bit less than you need. That need might just draw out of you the creative instincts that can make your business the next Grocery Game or **Nebraska Furniture Mart**.

Action Steps:

1. Exactly how much money do you need to start your business?
2. Can you restructure so that you can start with your own capital?
3. Anyone else that can help or partner with you?

#3 The Fear of Loneliness:
Just thinking about the subject I have come to realise that the main issue new business owners struggle with this not so much being alone and having all the attention on them but it is a question of have people around you that complement your skills in a relationship that suits your needs. That I believe is the craven in the heart of most entrepreneurs I have met!

The media depicts the successful business owner as a 'Self Made!' That is a deceptive and far from the truth title. No one becomes successful by themselves. It is simply impossible. At the other end of the scale of those who will make you successful are your clients who choose to purchase your products! They will have to communicate to you their needs, desires and wants and through that type of communication you have no chance of being lonely.

Let's face it; to a large extent if you set up a business; the buck stops with you at least for the most part. If you are the person with the idea, the key person and the one with the primary risk; the buck ought to stop with you.

It should never be a position you relinquish to others. This should create confidence rather than fear.

On the other hand there are so many people and organizations that will walk and work with you to ensure success and we will look at the best means of acquiring the help you need so that you do not feel lonely.

There are several reasons why we think we will be lonely:

1. **Not knowing everything:** We have a chapter on the subject but I will say a few things about it here.
   You are right; you do not know everything you need to know. Even Donald Trump does not know everything there is to know about properties in every country in the world. Does he? No! But what does he know? He knows enough to make him a multi-millionaire, he understands how his niche works and the strategic means for exploiting that niche.

   Although Warren Buffet is one of the richest men in the world and probably one of the most learned men on the earth on the subject of shares, and although each of his shares (Berkshire Hathaway) sell for around $170k; he still doesn't know about all the best businesses to buy in the world. But what does he know? He knows enough about certain types of shares that have made him a billionaire!

You see you are right; nobody knows everything there is to know. The point is that you just need to know enough. That "enough" is initially acquired by research and the rest comes when you start your business not when you are sitting at home waiting to know it all.

2. **Fear of making a catastrophic mistake:** I wish I could tell you "You will never make silly mistakes" If I did it would be a lie. Every business person will at some point especially in the beginning stages of their journey will make some silly mistakes. That is all part of the journey to success. Warren Buffet tells of the number of investments he made that were disasters and the ones he passed on that become very successful.

The problem sometimes is that many have not cultivated the attitude Sir Richard Branson expresses in his famous statement " Opportunities are like buses there is always another one coming along" There will always be the opportunity to make things right to get back up to try again; so why worry to the point of inactivity?
You will make mistakes but you will learn from them, grow from them and utilize those same mistakes by turning a catastrophe to a catalyst for success.

3. **Fear of not knowing what to do:**
   Again this causes a feeling of loneliness. Who wants to come to a point where you may not know what to do? However I have two things to say to put you at rest. Firstly have you ever thought how a nursing mother knows what to do when the new baby arrives? Sure she may have gone to antenatal classes (with the father of the child hopefully. I think men should get more involved in these things!) Where she learns from experienced nurses but there are always peculiarities that cannot be taught. How then does the woman know what to do

when those peculiarities show up? It is innate! In the same way I believe with your ability to conceive a business comes the ability to solve the problems relating to that business. Have you ever gone to ask for help and the person tells you to do exactly what you were thinking about? Yes how comes you did not do what you thought of; the answer is confidence.

Here is the deal; the more challenges you solve the more confident you become and the more you trust your own ability to know what to do. Secondly there is always help; a sounding board, a friend or colleague. We will now discuss those. You see; you are never alone!

So what are some of the sources that alleviate the loneliness a business owner may feel? Another way of saying this is where can a new business owner go to and obtain much needed advice?

1. **A Business Partner:** If you really do not want to "go it alone" then a business partner is always a good bet. Within it has a great deal of benefits; one of which is the elimination of loneliness. A business partner

does not need to have the same rights as you have in the business but they must share in the risks and bring complementary skills to the table.

A word of caution is that since this is not a loose relationship, the person must be tested first before you consider them as a partner. I would also go as far as saying the test must include one of a monetary nature.

Secondly, everything you agree on must be put into a legal document that you both sign. In this way you formalise the relationship; everyone knows where they are and it eliminates most of the problems that can arise in future especially when the business becomes financially successful.

2. **Coaching:** This can be in two forms One to One Coaching or Group Coaching. For a new business I suggest group coaching with ad hoc one to one coaching. The reason being that you will probably be with a group of people having the same experiences as you are having and the camaraderie that ensues from such relationships can completely transform the way you see your situation. Also the real value can be the amount to help and advice such a group

can offer. This totally removes; loneliness if you become an active participant.

The other values are the lower costs to the one to one coaching plus you can almost find group coaching available within every industry, so search on Google, Forums (this is also a great source for advice) . Industry Magazines or ask those already established within the field.

3. **Local Government Bodies:** There is www.sba.gov in the USA and numerous FREE Business Advice Centres in the UK. SBA also offers free mentoring programmes called SCORE Mentors. So depending on your country there is always credible free advice and mentoring that takes that lonely feeling away.

4. **Ask a friend:** Looking within your own network for someone who might be willing to help could solve the problem of being lonely. That person can act as a non-executive director and can often delay any reward to them for a specified future date. They could provide valuable, regular counselling to you that can aid your business. The beauty of this kind of relationship is that you can communicate

with the person over the internet or on the phone although meeting them face to face always provides a personal element to the experience.

Established business owners are always more than willing to contribute to a new business. It makes them feel more valued and offers them the opportunity to give back into the community.

All you need to do is ask you just don't know; they might say yes!

In conclusion I hope you realise that while there is a genuine concern about loneliness there are so many methods of circumventing those feelings and using the problems it creates as an opportunity to build meaningful relationships.

Action Steps:

1. Make a list of your strength and weaknesses so that you can find someone with complementary skills
2. Write a list of 5-10 people you know who are in business. Can they help you. Create your strategy to approach them. Ask if they can give you 30mins to 1 hour per month

3. Visit your local business advice agency – can they help.
4. If you want a partner; make a list of those you will consider. Write a list of criteria and what you are prepared to give the partner. Think about how the relationship could work.
5. Take action!

#4 "Fear of Fear of Losing Money"

Fear of losing money is one of the biggest hurdles for people who want to start their own business. Make no mistake about it; this form of fear is real. Fear is an emotion, and it is natural for human beings to feel fear. How a person handles fear is what determines raving success or utter failure. In fact, fear is a good thing; it can help you focus.

This chapter is going to focus about the fear of losing money - the reasons behind the fear, suggested solutions and an easy to follow action plan.

Reasons behind the Fear of Losing Money Loss Aversion- we are society that nearly equates to losing money as a failure. Naturally, we have an aversion to losing, as we do not want to see ourselves as a failure. However, ask any self-made millionaire how many times they failed and lost money. Most of them will tell you – many times.

The most important part is getting up, learning from the loss and trying again. Every failure has a hidden lesson that you must discover. Too Much At Risk- if you have too much money invested in a business venture, it is natural that you will be fearful of the outcome.

Furthermore, it is not the amount of money that gets you, but rather the amount of money in relation to your total assets that will fuel the fear. For example, $100,000 may cause sleepless nights for people who have a total asset value of $200,000. However, the same amount of money would be spare change for a person who has $10 million in assets.

Lack of Understanding- if you do not have sufficient understanding in relation to your possible business venture, then fear may overwhelm you. This is a perfectly natural response since it is related to "fear of the unknown". This is also a good thing, as it will protect you from a lot of misfortunes. On the downside, handling the fear poorly will also prevent you from succeeding.
Embarrassment- another reason why people have a fear of losing money is because when the word goes out, they do not want other people to think of them as poor. This is a rather a silly idea since no individual reached success without ever experiencing failure.
Suggested Solutions

To Remedy The Fear Of Losing

- **Money Management**- do not put all your eggs in one basket. Statistics state that on average, a person must fail two businesses before building a business that finally succeeds. Why not invest only one-third of your money so in case the venture fails, you will still have money to build two more.

- **Education**- building a successful business will require tons of education. You will not only need education related to your business venture, but also general business education.

- **Detachment**- as much as possible, try to detach yourself from your investment money. While it may be difficult to completely detach yourself from your money, but you can improve your detachment by telling yourself that you are only investing money that you can afford to lose; and make sure it's also true.

- **Strategy**- another way of shutting-out the fear of losing money is by keeping yourself busy so the emotion will not creep up on you. Just don't formulate a strategy for the sake of shutting-out the emotion. Make sure that your strategy is sound and measurable. Action Plan!

All this talk about roots and solutions in relation to the fear of losing money is almost worthless if we do not formulate an action plan. Therefore, below is a suggested working plan you might want to adopt.

- **Assess Your Assets**- before you even consider putting money to a business venture; make sure that you can afford to lose the money if ever the business flops. As suggested before, avoid putting all your eggs in one basket.

- **Assess Your Education** - honestly evaluate your education and understanding in relation to the possible business venture. If you feel you are lacking, then educate yourself by reading books or magazines, watching videos or attending seminars.

- **Adopt The Right Attitude**- think positively, but be prepared to fail. The most important thing is to learn from your failure and apply what you have learned to your next business venture.

- **Develop A System** - create a daily "things to do" or a daily system in relation to your overall strategy. By doing so, you will be avoiding the mistake of making a strategy just for the sake of shutting-out the fear, but also you will know that you are moving forward. Also, make regular assessments and re-adjust.

The fear of losing money is very real, but it does not have to be negative. You simply need to know how to harness the fear and better manage it. Keep in mind that successful people are not devoid of fear; they simply know how to deal with it and use it to their advantage.

Action steps
1. How much does your business need and why?
2. Write down 10 ideas you have for raising the funding your require
3. Choose the best 3 and start acting on them today
4. Can you implement any of the above ideas?

#5 Fear of The Current Economic Conditions

2014 has proven to be a challenging year for the American economy. The changes coming with the implementation of the Affordable Care Act as well as changes to immigration and monetary policy mean that things are likely to be more than a little unstable as the year presses on. If you are sitting on the economic side-lines because of downsizing, these are likely to be scary times for you. As you watch your savings dwindle, the stresses of everyday life simply mount up. Even if you're still employed, knowing that the economy could turn on your company at any time has to be stressful as well.

Why the Problem Exists

In some ways, the global economy is still shaking off the turmoil that erupted in 2008 and 2009, when the housing market collapsed, taking several large major banks with it and requiring billions of dollars in emergency assistance from the American government. While housing prices are slowly starting to ease their way back up, the simple fact is that things are nowhere near robust yet. Changes in 2014 began with the implementation of the Affordable Care Act. In the United States, the health sector accounts for almost $3 trillion each year, or about 18 percent of the total gross domestic product (GDP).

Any element that will bring significant change to that sector has major potential implications. While enrolment numbers have made it closer to what the government projected, it remains to be seen what will happen over the next six to twelve months, as patients begin using their new insurance. If the government and the private insurers can work together to ensure that the payment structure is sound, then these worries should ease. Immigration reform is another topic that will bring significant shifts to the economy, particularly on the employment front. As more momentum builds towards a larger granting of right for immigrants to work, the more supply there will be in the labor pool. This could mean that the drive to raise the minimum wage will abate, because there will be more people willing to work for $7.25 an hour.

As the debate between paying off the American national deficit and continuing the policy of infusing money into the economy in order to build jobs rages, the 2014 midterm elections will be very interesting. If the Republicans take the House and Senate, it will be difficult for Congress to pass bills that raise the minimum wage and boost job creation. This could have a significant impact on Americans who are looking for a new job.

Finally, the government's policies on high-risk mortgages have kept interest rates low, as the Federal Reserve's policy of buying bonds with risky mortgages and then guaranteeing them has reduced the amount of risk that lenders have significantly. However, it also represents a major taxpayer investment in loans that may default. As the Fed begins tapering this program back, it will be interesting to see how quickly mortgage rates spike and how quickly the sales of homes begin to drop.

How to Solve the Problem?

Just because the American economy is not doing well does not mean that there is no room for people to succeed. For example, Apple is doing as well as it ever has, moving into the online retail sales market to bolster the revenues that the iPad, iPhone and other technological toys are bringing in. So how can you take advantage of this?

- **Identify a product or service that people need**. What will people pay you to do? What service or product can you provide? Whether you are looking to provide online tutoring for writing or believe that you can run a plumbing company in your area better than the existing competition, there are always niches for growth.

- **Locate some seed capital.** If you have a great idea but simply lack the funds to put the whole thing together, there are more sources of money out there than there have ever been before. In addition to the traditional sources of funding, like banks, there are government organizations like the Small Business Administration that issue loans and grants for new businesses. Crowd-funding opportunities allow you to publicize your idea and then benefit from small investments that others make to help you get off the ground. If you have access to larger funders, hone your skills with presentations and make the case for your business.

- **Treat your business like a real job.** If you get the funding to get up and running, you have to treat what you're doing like it's a real full-time job. That means having a schedule when you work, conducting your business with the utmost professionalism, and marketing yourself every chance you get.

- **Believe in your idea.** If you have a concept that is sound, you will start to hear positive feedback relatively quickly. It may not be in the amount that you want, but a solid idea will take off with sound marketing and professional discipline from you as a business owner.

Action Steps

- Find a mentor. Bounce your business ideas off someone who has made money as an entrepreneur. Don't be defensive when you get a lot of feedback; instead, put it to work.
- Start a website. No successful business today is just a brick-and-mortar concern. Use tools like WordPress to set up a

basic free website and get yourself up and running.

- Learn all about social media. Given the amount of time that people spend on their smart phones and their social media accounts, your business must have its own Twitter and Facebook pages. Google+ is starting to take off as well, so take advantage of as many platforms as you can. Websites like Entrepreneur.com have daily news articles about trends in social media.
- Set up a working routine. Once you're committed to your business, you might not have the resources to set up your own office. While you're working from home, make sure that you work a set number of hours each day and meet a specific number of targets. It's easy to get distracted by daytime television and the refrigerator in the kitchen. The more discipline you show, the more success you can expect.

#6 Fear of Being Too Old To Start a Business Now!

Ray Kroc started McDonalds at the age of 52. Harland Sanders franchised KFC when he was 64. Steve Jobs brought his greatest innovations to Apple in his late 40s
<u>www.bellinghamherald.com</u>

I have heard a twenty five year old utter these words "I am too old to start a business" Equally I have heard the same phrase from a 45 year old. Older people in the age range of 50-65 even say the same things!
What is shocking today is that society discounts the aged and many young people think they have all there is to know and that the aged have nothing to offer but nostalgic myths!

The matter is compounded by those who are considering a business venture that lends itself to some physical activities like someone considering a sport based business. Being 20 is too old to start some sports and 50 years of age is absolutely a none-starter in some avenues. Yet I could show you <u>Ms. Ernestine Shephard</u> who has the body of a 28 year old but is 72 years of age. Or should we talk about

Roger Miller the Cameroon footballer who became the star of 1990 World Cup at the age of 38.

Whether it is the business of sport or that of website creation, many older people feel they are simply too old to pursue a business career.

Let's not forget that at the age of 45 and over you have distinct advantages that younger people do not have. I'll remind you of some of them:

- **You have the advantage of experience:** By the time anyone is in their 40's, 50's or 60's they would have accumulated so much life and business experience. I call it "Life Wealth" – it is basically knowledge and expertise that cannot be obtained overnight no matter how smart you are. This Life Wealth can be such a great ingredient to business success especially as it relates to what is known about people or a particular subject. More importantly if your area of business is what you have worked in; it is likely you are on to winner.

- **You have the advantage of having access to money:** At that senior age it is likely that you have been able to save up or have access to some retirement fund. Even if you don't have access to your own money you could know someone who does (See "Personal Network" point below). Anyone just starting out is unlikely to have such contacts and money.

- **You have the advantage of Personal Networks:** The question of Who You Know is still extremely relevant even in the internet world. Do not take lightly the personal contacts you have built up over many years it is a huge business advantage. Just imagine the contacts someone who has worked in marketing and sales would have after 15 years of service? Can that be leveraged in the new business? Absolutely yes! Think about how many people owe you favours that you can cash in on now. Most young people do not have that. You are at an advantage.

- **You have the advantage of "Testing":** What I mean by this is that over the years you have had the opportunity to test certain assumptions and realise what works and what doesn't. Consider the amount of money to be saved from the testing you have witnessed over the years you have worked! Invariably anyone starting a new business must test their hypothesis over a period. This may cost money or at least valuable time that you do not need to spend. One very important point is that the accumulation of testing, personal networks, experience and access to money will help you create a great business plan. Now; since most of the tests have been carried out all you need to do is plan and execute for success.

I realise that some older men and women would need to overcome certain challenges which are not insurmountable. It really does depend on your attitude and approach to each of those areas. With the right actions and coaching you can use what appears as hindrances to become a footstool to success.

You may need to:

- **Get some business knowledge:** If all you have done is work for someone else it would not hurt to read some books and attend some courses on business basics, entrepreneurship and leadership. Every business person needs these. If you feel the basics are way too low for the experience you have gained then go for an advanced or catch up level. Be aware that running your own business is very different from working for someone else!

- **Get some social media knowledge:** I say this with caution because I have discovered that whilst younger people know how to use social media platforms for fun many lack the knowhow of using the media to generate money, grow a business and market for growth. So do not be intimidated. Besides, the way technology works these days you can find your way around most things if you are capable of sending emails.

- **Get back the freedom to take risks:** every business attracts an element of risk no matter how well you plan. Whilst some of the aspects of business discussed above have the capacity to eliminate some of the risks associated with a new business an older person will be required to take some calculated risks. The problems start when the older person has more to lose than a single person who only has to think about him/herself. They may have some financial commitment, children still at home or some other personal issue. In my book **"How To Transition From Employee To Self Employed"** I dealt with the issue of taking risks and involving the family. The more you involve those that could be affected in the process the more likely they are to offer support. This then reduces pressure and allows you to focus on the business. You will need to take some risk and what is required of you is not to completely eliminate every conceivable risk but to limit their effects as much as you can. If therefore you have created an effective business plan; there will be no need for fear or worry

- **Get a good business plan:** Unless you are a serial entrepreneur you should put together a comprehensive business plan for the purpose of starting and running your business. Sensible people realise the importance of having a business plan but for those who feel they would rather not have one; you are missing out on the opportunity to fail on paper; the opportunity to discover specifically what your business needs; the opportunity to attract funding plus the opportunity to interest serious people to join your business venture.

In conclusion I hope I have been able to persuade you that you are not too old to start but that you are actually in a better opportunity of starting a business than those who are younger then you.

We are often likely to focus of the negative instead of considering the many positive factors we have going for us. You must change your focus and concentrate on what you have rather then what you lack. Bear in mind that you can become much more productive simply because you are older and wiser!

If you are interested in starting a business and you don't, at the end your life you will be filled with regret. Remember the saying *"Our biggest regrets are not for the things we have done but for the things we haven't done"* — *Chad Michael Murray*

Action steps

1. Write down the product you want to sell and those that have the pain it solves. This will help you clarify where you are going and contribute towards your business planning process
2. List all the business contacts and those who perceive could help you in the launch process of your business.
3. List the skills you think you are missing out on. Speak to the people on the list above and ask them for help. If they are unable to help ask them to sign post you to coaching, forums or courses that can be of help.
4. Start putting together a business plan. There are so many books on writing a business plan you can get from Amazon and other online retailers. Have a look at my own too if you like, it is called **"How To Write Your First Business Plan": With Outline and Templates Book (First Timer's Guide:)**

#7 The Fear of Not Knowing Enough!

It may shock you to know that no business book written by any man can ever teach all you need to know to run you own business. You can take this to bank! If one book had all the solutions; why do you have 3, 4, 8, 10 books on the same subject on your book shelf.

The real deal is that hopefully each book you read will build on the other; connect the dots and push you further down the track to success.

In the same way, you are right to think you do not know all there is to know about the business you want to start. But that in no way signifies you do not know enough! There is a difference. Let me explain.

Every business is like going on a journey. You can plot a map of your 500 mile journey; see what it looks like on paper or even generate all the satellite images that relate to the journey but as you take the first 10-20 miles you will quickly realise that some things will be different about that journey. It could be the weather change making the difference; the people in the vehicle with you or even the car you are factors that can make the difference. All the variations in the journey will not prevent you from arriving at the correct destination.

So it is when running a business. You must know as "much as you can" to help you get started but you will never know every minute detail of how everything will work out in practice. That is why your business plan must be flexible enough to accommodate changes as they arise.

Many people have confused not knowing everything with not knowing enough and have chosen to wait until they know everything before they start a business. I have news for you – you are likely to wait forever!

Let me help you out by asking a question; "what are the key aspects of the business you need to know before you start your own business?"

1. **What are you offering:** Or what can you offer? Do you have some knowledge that people are after or will want? Danny Inny from Firepole Marketing asks a relevant question - Can you teach someone new in the business what they may need to know

for about 20 minutes. Basically define what you are offering

2. **Who are those who have the 'pain' it solves?:** The next aspect of the business is the market research that helps you determine the people you are able to help or those likely to purchase your product. Would they consider your solution as an 'aspirin' or 'vitamin' product? Meaning would they see what you have as something they need immediately or what they can do without. This is able to determine your sales potential and equally your market size.

3. **How am I going to reach them?:** Where are they, where do they go to buy, who are they buying from right now, why are they buying from your competitors etc.?

4. **How much will they pay?:** How much are they currently paying for similar products, would they pay more, are they price sensitive etc.?

5. **How much will it cost?** what will it cost to start and run the business, do you have enough money etc.?

Everything else is just details that can be worked out. In simple terms your business plan will likely encompass the 5 areas outlined above. So as discussed in another chapter, once you have your business plan well researched you know enough to start. Don't limit yourself by what you do not know; use what you DO know. Again, there are so many books on writing a business plan you can get from Amazon have a look at my own too if you like it is called **"How To Write Your First Business Plan": With Outline and Templates Book (First Timer's Guide:)**

In conclusion I want to give you with three thoughts to consider:

1. **Corridors of opportunity:** I first learned about the Corridor of Opportunity from Brian Tracy many years ago. He said that they are so many opportunities available for someone but they will only be accessed as the person walks down the corridor. Those doors will only open to the person already walking the corridors. If the individual chooses to stay outside them they will never experience the opportunities locked in behind the doors of the corridor. In the same way, until you start your business some of the answers you want will

not come because they are only available to those who have taken the first step of starting.

Let me explain it another way. As an author of many books on Amazon, people ask me to teach them to write and publish books. The very first thing I do is to test them. I ask them to go on Amazon and purchase a .99c book on how to write; I tell them to come back to me once they have read the book. Most never return. My test proves they were never serious. I could have wasted my time with them. But those who come back, I then spend time with and teach. I was not going to show time wasters how to make money!

2. **Good Samaritan:** (Quick summary of this Biblical story told by JESUS) A man was on his way but unfortunately waylaid by robbers. Many people passed him but one unlikely person who was a Samaritan stopped to help him. Do you realise that from this one story the organisation called The Samaritans have been working and helping people internationally!

   If that man was not there going about his business he will not have the help he enjoyed and the international organisation that have been responsible for being there for 1000's of needy people with problems like bereavement, suicide, depression would have no help!

So now let me apply the story to us - The quality of help you receive at the beginning of your business is lower than what you will receive once you start making some profit. The types of people ready and willing to join a new business is generally lower than those who will join once you get going. The number of people willing to join and work for Facebook, Google and YouTube are much more today than it was 6 years ago. Just imagine if all these businesses were waiting until they knew everything that could have happened or if the man in the story had sat at home afraid because of the danger of the journey.

3. **Your waiting game is costing other people:** It is said in the USA that small businesses are the biggest employers. Threats will be the case for nearly every country on earth. That means that if the economic condition in the world is to change, small businesses are the catalyst to precipitate that change. Yet 1000's of

small business owners with great ideas are sitting on the fence thinking they don't know enough. Sadly they have not realised how powerful they are but are still waiting for the power and authority to act. The waiting game is costing people employment they could gain from you, it is costing your nation of the input you could have in to the economy and moreover it is delaying the world from coming out of economic gloom.

You see you have no further need to sit on the fence but rather take action that will help you create a high performance business that will change you and your family, your community and also the international community.

Action Steps

1. Write down exactly the information you think you are missing. If nothing comes to mind, test your product with your target group and ask for feedback
2. Can you get it by reading or attending courses or coaching? Can you get the help you need within the next 7 days
3. Now that you have the information what is stopping you?

4. Then start testing your product again. If you get the all clear start the business by selling to a larger group

#8 Fear of Competition

A competitive market is defined as *(Competitive market) In economics, competition is the rivalry among sellers trying to achieve such goals as increasing profits, market share, and sales volume by varying the elements of the marketing mix: price, product, distribution, and promotion* - Web definitions

I have heard is said "Everybody is doing what I am thinking about doing" or "There are so many people in that market" or "My idea will get lost in that huge market"

When someone thinking about starting a business makes those statements they are simply saying – Even though I want to start my business I am afraid of established competition!

It is proper to put a competitive market into the right perspective so that we do not under/over estimate the value of competition and also that a new business can appreciate the fact that there is always room within a competitive market.

I want to start by giving you 4 clear advantages for any new business thinking of going into a competitive market.

Advantages of a competitive market

- **Established market:** It is great news to anyone starting a business to understand there is room for growth within that particular market because it has millions or thousands of willing and active buyers/sellers. Who want to go into a dead market or a shrinking market for that matter? Competitive markets smell of opportunities to sell your products and market money because it is very active.

    Let's take the Weight Loss market. Is that competitive? Sure! Every other website and Facebook page is trying to sell you some form of weight loss product. What does this mean? There are thousands of people dealing with this challenge and suppliers are there to meet that demand. Unless people radically change their life style, that market will continue to grow. The more obese people become the larger the market and then more competitive it will be.

- **Easy to come up with an idea:** Simply improve what exists. When operating within a competitive market there are always a plethora of products already in existence with some doing very well. A new business does not need to scratch their brain too hard as to start from the beginning. Within such a market it is easier to find an existing saleable product and improve on it.

- **Easy to raise money for such a product**: Investors/Funders find it easier to understand a business directed towards a competitive market because there is so much information about it. People generally only invest in what they understand. Furthermore coming up with a plan that wants to average 2% of a multibillion dollar market is of better interest to an investor that a business selling products within a "Don't know who" market.
Hence it is easier to raise funding for a product within a competitive market that has developed a niche.

- **Forces you to become more creative:** As much as we dislike competition it can become the vital force that propels creativity. When you are operating within this market you have to dig deep to come up with a product that sets you apart from the rest. So whether you develop on an existing product or create one from scratch you will use much of your creative juices. Invariable this is good for your customers and further enables the market to remain competitive for others too!

The Secret

Rather than talk about disadvantages I will talk about the secrets that will invariably deal with the disadvantages of selling a competitive product into a competitive market.

From my knowledge of the soft drinks market the two top brands – Coke (Coca-Cola) and Pepsi are the market leaders. There are 100other drink manufacturers competing for the same market. With that said; as big as the Coke brand is not everyone drinks Coke regularly. At the time of writing this page I am struggling to remember the last time I bought a bottle of Coke, even though I bought a drink this morning. The point *I* am making is that no matter how dominate a particular brand is not everyone uses it.

Recently in the UK a new juice drink was started by two guys straight out of University it was called Innocence. With little funding and loads of zeal they made the business into a multimillion dollar business within a few years and recently sold to Coca-Cola. Consider this they carved out their own market within that competitive market and made a fortune out of it.

So secret #1 Find a niche within that market: Competitive markets are generally dominated by aggressive brands that can squeeze you out of the market. But the self-employed always have the advantage of reaching clients in such a way that major brands cannot. Use this advantage and capitalize on it.

This example will help you understand the niche market I am talking about. Think about the Weight Loss market; there are diets, clothing, vitamins and classes. Exercise machines, coaches, etc just to name a few. This section has subsections and variations. So you might have Zumba and Calypso classes and several other classes directed towards particular parts of body and so on.

Although you have all of these present in the market a niche could be Weight Loss of the over 50's or Abs for the over 40's – those are specifically targeted towards a particular group of people. A niche avoids the general market but goes for a specific one. So niche your product.

Secret #2 Take advantage of the competitive market by niche marketing your product. The other scary part of working in a competitive market is the marketing that needs to taken before the new brand becomes known.

Following on from having a niche the marketing efforts become easier and much more targeted. Gone were the days of putting an ad in the local paper and hoping it gets everyone. You are not selling to everyone but a specific audience.

Your efforts can reach the people to whom is it aimed by using mediums like Facebook, marketing on specific niche related forums and so on. You no longer need the machine approach but one 2 one targeted approach to marketing.

In conclusion I hope you are rest assured that the competition is actually a good thing and that working within a competitive market can make you more inspired and creative plus provide high quality services to your clients.

In effect you are able to turn that fear into a springboard for success!

Action Steps

1. Who are the major players in your industry? What products/services are they offering?
2. What are their weaknesses?
3. What gap in the market can you fill and who are those with the 'pain' you can relieve?
4. How do you plan to reach this demographic?

#9 Fear of Taking Risks

"Be wise enough not to be reckless, but brave enough to take great risks."
— Frank Warren

Within the business plan writing circles it is always said that one should write about the risks associated with the business within the executive summary along with what your plans are to mitigate those risks. They say the worst thing any entrepreneur seeking investment can do is to say; "There are no risks associated with the business".

I have said the above to make you understand that no matter how well you conduct your research, take advice, pray and get the best team together; there will still be an element of risk associated with starting a new business otherwise everybody would be doing it and we would need to learn nothing.

What you must realise is that even when it looks like things in the business are not working, that is the time for you to get your best possible education.

Risks are part and parcel of running a business and the research process should help you take calculated risks as opposed to uncalculated ones.

So what are 'Calculated and Uncalculated Risks'?

Uncalculated Risks – are risks people take without considering the consequences and end results.

Calculated Risks – are risks taken with your eyes wide open meaning; after conducting research and received valuable information that helps you decide what the final outcomes may be. When you hear stories of people who lost it all; much of the time they gambled rather than took calculated risks.

When you invest your last penny into a business your neighbour promised you will gross 500% in a month; it is not taking calculated risks but plain gambling and greed.

Calculated risked are those taken after research dictates what the final outcome may be and then proceeding with confidence and courage knowing we are well prepared. It may consider the worst case scenario but realised even if it happens it will not be the end of the story rather the beginning of a better one. Again a calculated risk will look at the best possible outcome too knowing all necessary steps have been taken to mitigate all negative circumstances.

Calculated and Uncalculated risks are one thing the consequences of risk is another.

Lets us explore this for a moment.

Consequences of Risk:

Non Action – whenever someone thinks about the consequences of risk, we tend to focus on negative outcomes of what goes wrong from the action taken. things go wrong. We need to remember that non-action posses a bigger consequence than actions that go wrong. There is a saying that it is easier to control a horse in motion than one which is lying down.

Much of the regrets people have at the end of their lives are not for the actions they took but the risks they did not take, the speeches they did not make and opportunities they failed to create!

Non-action is a deadly disease loaded with regret.

Actions that go wrong: This is most familiar for people. Friends and family can tell you of people they know who took the risk of starting a business and discovered how they lost everything they owned. Others have their little personal stories of what went wrong.

What many fail to realise is that, starting business is not a 100 metre sprint but a marathon! In a marathon I am told that there are times your body gets so tired that you almost want to give up but the months of training kicks in to ensure you reach the finishing line.

Just like being tired in a marathon; no matter how bad failures seem they are the fertilizers that make success possible. When we sit on the fence and avoid taking risks simply because we loath the idea; how will success ever come? When you take a calculated risk and it goes wrong you will have learnt so many valuable lessons that going further down the journey of business ensures success.

Truth about risk: If you want to run your business by taking uncalculated risks then you have a lot to be worried about. But if you are taking calculated risks then you must free your mind from the fear of worry because the two are clearly not the same.

Another point to remember is that there is not one single business I know about that does not involve an element of risk. In practice businesses have peaks and troughs; ups and downs; great decisions that produce an immense amount of fruit and not so great decisions that are costly.

Let's face it; an element of uncertainty is actually a recipe for creativity. If you do not know the future 100% you are likely to do much more in the present to mitigate adverse events that may happen in the future; thereby drawing upon your creativity!.

Again, working in an environment that involves an element of calculated risk ensures you become more competitive. You are likely to work harder knowing that your competitors are firing on all cylinders. Remember that competition breeds better products and better products make your clients happier.

Finally; who wants to have regrets in the future? It is better to take a risk now and have it all go wrong than to sit on the fence in fear and anxiety. Take calculated risks; the opportunity cost for not doing so are riskier that you can ever imagine!

After hearing the truth about taking risks and knowing that most entrepreneurs are risk averse that is why they have money and only take calculated risks; I want to give you 3 alternatives to explore when starting a business:

Although many talk about 'Going it alone'- meaning starting a business by yourself; in reality there is nothing as such. I say that because even when you are running a business alone you will still work with external individuals who contribute work to the success of your business i.e. external contractors. Therefore in practice there is no pure 'Go it alone entrepreneur'.

However there are some types of business structure where working together is much more pronounced and some might consider these as a much more viable method of starting a business. So let me briefly outline the 4:

1. **Partnership:** This is where you set up the business with one or more individuals. You share risks and decision

making plus decide how profits will be split too. The idea removes loneliness as well as further distributes the calculated risks involved in running a business.

2. **Franchise:** This is a system of business where to take on a 'tried and tested' brand. You get full support from the head office and you simply follow a laid down route that has worked several times. Franchise by nature can be expensive because of the support and the lower risks involved. Also franchises are extremely restrictive in nature. If you would like to put your stamp on a business then a franchise may not be for you. One of the major benefits are risk reduction and support.

3. **A Buy-in:** What I mean by this is where you buy shares in an existing going concern and take on the role of co-owner. Similar to partnerships but here we are talking about buying shares within a Company or LLC. Obvious advantages are that you are joining an existing team of people, a profitable business (hopefully) and a going concern where risks are shared. You could buy-in

for a price that enables you to become an equal shareholder with the founder.

4. **Buy An Existing Business**: There are many organisations that start good businesses with the view of selling them further down the line. People reach retirement age and sell their businesses or some change their life style and sell going concerns. Buying an existing business further reduces the calculated risk of starting from scratch. Since such a concern will become yours; you will be free to make all the changes you desire and make the business more suitable to you. One drawback is the cost of acquisition and product/market knowledge.

I think you now have some rounded information about the fear of taking risks and I am sure making the right decision that suits you will not be as difficult as you originally thought!

Actions:

1. What part of the business process makes you anxious?
2. Do you know enough about these areas?

3. Read at least one good book about that area.
4. Now that you know the truth, don't let anything stop you!

#10 Fear of What People Have Said

Recently I was teaching a group of people about 'Success in the workplace, setting and achieving goals and having accountability partners'; when someone said "What if you share your dreams with people who are negative?" My reply was that negative people should only hear your dreams once and never share it with them again until/unless they change.

Shamefully the effect of negative comments by family members (including parents), people in authority, close friends and the like; have stopped many fledging entrepreneurs from starting their businesses.

Much of the poison injected into would be business owners include:

"Remember that most businesses fail"

"Why do you want to give up your secure job?"

"What will happen if you lose all that money?"

"Think about all the wasted effort"

"I am sure there are better ways to spend your time"

"You are too young you still have time"

"I think you are too old to be taking such risks"

The list is endless. It all works together to cradle the kind of fear that incapacitates the entrepreneur!

So the question is 'What can you do to remove this poison from your system plus what attitude can you employ to keep such talk out of your life in future?'

Let's explore these now:

How to remove negative poison:

1. **Be responsible for your thoughts:**
   There is a saying that you cannot stop a bird flying over your head but you sure can stop the bird from nesting in your head. You may not be able to stop some negative comments coming your way but you can stop them staying within your heart!
   If you dwell on their negative comments and opinions long enough it will produce for you the realities you do not want.

Your response should be 'I don't have to dwell on what you said; after all I am in control of what goes on in my own mind'

2. **Don't discuss future dreams:** It is surprising to me that people return to the same individual who has given negative comments. It is almost as though we need the validation of a negative person or perhaps we are trying to prove to them how wrong they are. All of which are completely unnecessary. Once someone has proved their position to you; that person should no longer be privy to your dreams, vision and goals.

3. **Understand them:** What I mean here is that by understanding why they think the way they do you are in a better position to decline their offers of negative suggestion.

   Let us assume a family member went into business and lost all they owned but instead of getting up and trying again they simply go back to a 9-5 job and stayed in it. This type of person can tell you all businesses fail so why bother. Understanding where that perspective originates allows you to discount what they say without any guilt whatsoever.

4. **Cut them off:** Someone once said 'You don't chose your family but sure can chose your friends' Perhaps it is harder to stop talking to a negative family member but it is possible to cut off negative friends.
Remember that destructive criticism is like poison to your system. Why do you want to keep digesting negative comments? Cut these people off and say your occasional hellos!

Now that we are aware of how to remove the negative poison we need to cultivate an atmosphere that produces a 'You Can Do It' mindset, true motivation and discipline. All of these will enable us to keep negative talk out of our lives in future.

1. **Cultivate relationships with successful business owners**: I used to have an impression that seeing a successful business person would be like waiting for a bus that never arrives. That is so far from my experience. I have

found them to be the approachable, nicest and most willing to help.
Having relationships with a successful business owner that can mentor you is a key strategy to take you out of negative belief into a relationship that feeds you with the right kind of information. For those wondering how this relationship can be started, visit your local Chamber of Commerce or its equivalent.

2. **Join a coaching group:** I am shocked that most entrepreneurs lack the understanding of the intrinsic value of a coaching group as a means of speeding up their learning curve towards success. Join a local group you can physically attend or one online that can be attended via a webinar. Coaching groups range in their approach but have many similarities. Most engage with people of similar interests and dedication coming together for the success of all. It is generally facilitated by an experienced person and you will receive support from colleagues and the facilitator.

3. **Be consistent:** In his book the 15 Laws of Growth, John C. Maxwell talks about

the law of Consistency as the most important law. Although it sounds boring you must consistently keep negative people out of your life by intentionally doing just that.

Limit the time spent in their company, limit dialogue and avoid conversations about your future.

4. **Read books on successful start-ups:** Immerse yourself in literature that provides the impetuous to remain consistent, motivated and disciplined. Books carry within them the ability to impart truth like nothing else. Read for at least 30mins a day!

Action steps

1. Make a list of all the negative people you have around you.
2. Which ones will you cut off?
3. Find and join a coaching group
4. Develop a relationship with at least one successful entrepreneur

Conclusion

Now at least you have read about some of the common fears that have kept people from taking steps forward. Also I have given you solutions and action steps that will get you up and moving towards your quest of starting your own business.

Although I am available and do offer some support; it is up to you now. You can either go for it or make your dream come true or agree with what you have read yet take no action.

Both scenarios will have an outcome within the next 6-12 months!

I appeal to you take action! Use this book as a guide. Read and read it again especially when you are feeling down and then take action. You future depends on the action you take in the present!

Thank you so much for reading my book. I hope you really liked it.

As you probably know, many people look at the reviews on Amazon before they decide to purchase a book. If you liked the book, could you please take a minute to leave a review with your feedback?

You can review this book here on Amazon:

60 seconds is all I'm asking for, and it would mean the world to me. Thank you so much,

Boomy Tokan,

T: +44 7932 394620

E: boomy@startyourownbusinessacademy.com

W: www.startyourownbusinessacademy.com

#: @boomybizbooks

FREE Bonus

How To Start Your Own Business In 30 Days"

Hey ... If you would like to learn how to start and run a "High Performance" business; then download this FREE guide. It will also show you how to start making money from your business within 30 Days!

"How To Start Your Own Business In 30 Days"

Copy and paste in your browser:
www.startyourownbusinessacademy.com/freedownload1

Enjoy

Other Books by Boomy Tokan

"How To Write Your First Business Plan": With Outline and Templates Book (First Timer's Guide:)

Introduction & Chapter 1

In this book, I am going to teach you how to write two (2) types of business plans. The first one is a Comprehensive Business Plan Template and the second, a Power Point Business Plan. (I'll explain more in a moment)

Let me start by making two statements:

If you are just starting out in business, you need a business plan because of all the instructions and knowledge you will gain from going through education.

Writing a business plan is easy; at least it is easier than most people think. The problem lie in the manner business plans are perceived and portrayed by many institutions. Most have made the process intimidating for those who want to have a plan but do not want to be bothered with the plethora of business jargons that have been overemphasized in the business plan writing process.

My advice is - dispense with frivolities and write a well researched plan, the rest are details! The most important element of a business plan is the content not the jargon!

Ok let's get started!

The Comprehensive Business Plan Template

Generally speaking, most comprehensive business plans have the same information in them. They may have been given other titles but the basic format and requirements are similar. Hence the template I am giving you may not be the exact format you may have received from your local business adviser or accountant but the information within it will be the same. Also the format I am giving you has been tried and tested and I have personally used it to raise thousands for many of my clients.

The Five Parts of a Business Plan

Think about your hand. It has five fingers, right (hopefully)? Or just imagine you have five fingers. In the same way I want you to know that there are five parts to a business plan:

1. The Summary; also called "Executive Summary" or "Introduction"

2. The Marketing Plan

3. Operations Plan

4. Financial Plan

5. Appendices

These are the names I have used and it is easy for me to remember them. If at the end of the book you feel you want to call them something else then feel free to do so. The only proviso is that if you are trying to reach other people with the plan, they need to be familiar with or understand the terms you give the plan.

What Does Each Name Stand For:

1. **The Marketing Plan** – "What I Want To Do" - What type of business are you wanting to start?

What market do you want to start your business in? Who do you want to cater to?

2. **The Operation Plan** – "How I Am Going To Do It" – What kind of business structure do I need for this enterprise? Who do I need to network with? Do I need a mentor?

3. **The Financial Plan** – "What It Will Cost To Do It" - What are the costs of production, cost of sales or monthly expenses? How much profit will the business make in 12 months?

4. **Appendices** – "Additional Supportive Information" - like letters of intent, letters of recommendations, CV etc

5. **The final part which is the first one or two pages of your plan is the "Summary" or "Executive Summary".** Which is the summary of all the above 4 (Marketing Plan, Operations Plan, Financial Plan and Appendices). The general advice given is that this section must be written last and I agree to

that. You will understand more as we build up the business plan.

Once you understand this then you are ready to progress to the next stage. ....

Book Title: Business Funding Secrets: *How To Get Small Business Loans, Crowd Funding, Loans From Peer To Peer Lending, Government Grants and Personal Funding Ideas; Book*

If you want to know the truth about raising money for your business this book is for you.

If you are having a tough time raising the money you want for your business this book is for you too.

If you are not sure where to go to get the kind of funding you need for your business this book is just what you need.

After many years of helping businesses of various kinds raise the money they want, I have laid out in print all that you need to know about raising money for your start-up business! .

Read Introduction & Chapter 1
Introduction

I want to start by making a bold statement "There is more funding available than needed by Start-up Businesses"

Many start-up businesses convince themselves that the reason why it is difficult to get the money they need is because of scarcity. Nothing could be so far from the truth. Let me give you an example. When I worked for an organisation that gave loans to start-up businesses, they always had money for the businesses they believed would succeed and they usually rejected and gave a hard time to those businesses they felt would under-perform.

The problem is not scarcity but the lack of understanding the psychology for raising business finances.

Facts

"Business money is out there to be claimed, yet every year we receive stories of piles of cash sitting in accounts and not being invested. It's not because you don't need the cash, but it's because navigating through the grants jungle can have you wishing you still had your good job back".
http://www.startups.co.uk/grants-for-starting-a-business.html

Many people come to a raising finances seminar and at the back of their minds is this statement, "Give me the list of funders and I'll be on my way." The truth is that if you had a list of funders without understanding, it will be like giving a learner driver a Ferrari sports car. Occasionally they will drive the car on the road but they are more likely to crash than to survive the next 10 miles.

Understanding how to approach funders, knowing how to turbo-charge your business idea, presenting yourself well and finding solutions to all the hindrances on the way are much more important than having a long list of funding sources alone. So I have left that to the final part of the chapter. That is where I will tell you the various sources of funding and their requirements.

What the major players say:

Huw Morgan, Head of Business Banking for SMEs at HSBC Commercial Banking UK, agrees. He says HSBC looks at each business on a case-by-case basis when deciding whether to lend. "When making lending decisions we are looking to support firms with good cash flow management, a strong balance sheet, a sound business plan, a well-balanced management team, a good business record, and who are looking to develop and grow."

Neil Mackay of Advantage Business Angels suggests "you need to put some real effort into preparing a business plan: not a consultant template driven one but a well thought out document. Particular emphasis should be placed on sales and the plan should be less than 10 pages of A4".

http://www.sage.co.uk/business-potential/start-your-business/how-to-raise-finance-for-your-business.html

This book is written to help start-up and other newly established businesses understand the intricacies of raising money and position them to be able to leverage their ideas better and attract the required funding.

For easy reference I have split the book into 5 key sections:

1.   Answers to common, sensible questions about raising money for their business

2.   Why start-up fails to get the funding they require and the necessary solutions

3.   How to make your business fundable

4.   Understanding the psychology of investors

5.   Where is the money?

I have endeavoured to make this book as practical as possible, not leaving out any information that can be of help. Over the years I have helped many businesses raise finances from hundreds to thousands of dollars. Therefore my desire is that this book will help you along your journey to raising finances. The most important message I want to pass on to you as you begin reading the book is – Take Action Today!

Chapter 1: Answers to Common, Sensible Questions about Raising Money for Your Business

Anyone who has raised any amount of money for a business understands the pressure and the amount of time it can take to actually get the money in the bank. What I want to do first is to answer some of the common questions about raising money for your business:

1. How long does it take to get the money?: In every group I have delivered a lecture on raising money someone always asks me how long it takes from application process to receiving money from the bank. Unless you already have a great credit score and you are going to a bank that likes your account, then the average wait time is anywhere between 3-18 months. Somebody says, "What?" Yes 3-18 months! In some cases, it can even take over two years.

Knowing this information is really important because it means you need to plan in advance for your funding drive. Many people put themselves under pressure by applying for money exactly when they need it. Funders are very wary of people under such pressures because they appear to lack the ability to plan ahead and if that is the case how could they possibly plan for a business!

2. Does a good idea guarantee or equate to getting funding? No. What guarantees getting the funds you need is a good idea that is presented well. A good idea alone may get you nothing. What many new businesses may not know is that there are always many good ideas at the same time! I know by experience that everyone thinks they have the best idea and rightly so, otherwise you will have no imputes to go out and get the funding you need. But the reality is that some funders can have in excess of 1000 applications every month!

3. Do I need to get funders to sign a confidentiality agreement? A few years ago I met with a man called John Oram who produces valve music amplifiers; expensive stuff!. In a life changing conversation, he told me that when he gets an idea it seems to come in a complete package. He also told me that he believes he is not the only one that

gets the same idea at the same time. I asked him how he knew he was not the only one that had the same idea. His answer was shocking. He said that on many occasions he worked with people from different countries and they seemed to know intricate details of equipment that had never been manufactured. When he asked them how they got the idea the time and date mentions was the exact time and date he also received the idea! Amazing I told him that divine download was from GOD. If people separated by 100's miles can have the same ideas, you can begin to understand the problem with confidentiality agreements.
Some else can walk into the same funder with an idea similar to yours. Any way; funders hate to sign such documents. It puts them in a difficult position. To be frank with you, I will never sign such an agreement and when I was working for an advisory agency, we were told never to sign them because it could result in lawsuits.

Don't worry about the bad stories you hear of someone infringing another person's copyright; it only happens on rare occasions. If you think someone is likely to steal your idea do not even approach the person for funding!

4. How many meetings would I have to go to before I get the money? You will have has many that are necessary. But if you follow the ideas in this book you should reduce the number of meeting to the minimum. Honestly the number of meetings has to be judged on a case by case basis.

Initially there will be a flurry of going back and forth because there is likely to be issues the funders are not pleased with.

I must tell you this in my experience of placing business plans to funders I have never come across a complete business plan. I have come across very good business plans but never satisfied with every single detail of the plan. Besides you need to get used to the fact that all funders have different requirements and you will need to tailor your plan to their rules.

5. How many funders would I need to approach? One answer is as many as possible. The other is if you do your research properly an average of 5-10 funders should do it. Do your research and then choose a few that are likely to fund your idea. If I go to a funder that is likely to fund my type of business and they reject my application, they would likely give reasons for doing so and if I take onboard their suggestions – I increase my chances all the way! Raising money is not pop lunch but a strategic approach is essential!

6. How long should my business plan be?
There is no hard and fast rule as to the length of a business plan. However the Business Plan must look the part! Meaning if you are looking for $30,000 it must be obvious to the funders simply by the physical appearance or electronic copy of the plan that it is worth what is being sort! So here are some guiding principles in my opinion: if you want to raise $5000 I suggest at least a 12 page plan; raising $10,000, I suggest at least 15-20pages; raising $20,000 – $50,000 I suggest at least 25-50pages; raising $100,000, I suggest at least 100pages. I hope you get the picture. No one in their right mind will give $100,000 from a one or two page business plan unless you are Alan Sugar or Richard Branson!

"70 Public Speaking Tips"

Has been written to give individuals the tools and techniques to overcome the fear that limits them from delivering great speeches. **Boomy Tokan** reveals the how-to's of effective Public Speaking, and reveals how anyone can learn and implement them.
For all who need to make presentations in the workplace, at school or an event and expects someone to listen, ***70 Public Speaking Tips provides an insider's guide on how to***

present effectively
You will receive the exact steps needed to create a speech that will keep your audience engaged. The book is easy to follow, inspiring to read and designed to motivate you to become the best speaker you never thought you could be!

Topics covered include:
- Why You Need This Skill
- **Why some people have the fear of speaking in public. – It's origin and development**
- Psychology of public speaking (Part 1) - The internal dialogue of the person that hates public speaking.
- **Psychology of public speaking (Part 2) - The internal dialogue of the 'Successful' public speaker**
- How to overcome fear, stage fright and shyness of Public Speaking
- **Public Speaking exercises that will change you into a great speaker forever**
- 10 Tips that will help you captivate an audience
- **The Ultimate Public Speaking Preparation 'The 7 Most Do's' – How to prepare**
- How to choose an engaging topic and incorporate relevant stories
- Foods **which aid better Public Speaking**
- The Biggest Secret is the 'Secret of Practicing'

Read Introduction & Chapter 1

Introduction

The ability to speak in public confidently, articulately, and in a manner that enables others to completely comprehend what has been said, is of immense value to everyone who possesses it!

It was not until I was in college that it dawned on me that I had mastered public speaking to a proficient level.

I noticed that every time the tutor told us we had an assignment that would require a presentation, 99% of the class would complain and lobby the tutor to scrap the presentation aspect of the course work. I often sat there wondering why this took place all the time. It dawned on me that most of the students hated public speaking and, as the famous line goes, most people fear public speaking more than they fear death!

If this is your sentiment, I am about to change your fear into confidence for good.

Read on!

Once I realized my perception about the students was correct, I went about making my life easier! From that day, whenever we had course work that required a presentation, I would tell my group: "You guys do all the work. When it is ready, give it to me and I'll make the presentation." They would look so relieved! And so they would do all the work and I would read the report and present it. I thought this was a win-win deal; I got out of doing all the research and they got off doing the presenting!

It was only as I grew older that I realized we both lost. I did not learn administration and research in my earlier academic career (something I had to re-learn later in life), and they failed to master their fear of public speaking!

The other thing I began to grasp was that, contrary to what many people believe, public speaking can be learnt by EVERYONE! Rather than master the art of public speaking, many have mastered the art of public speaking "avoidance."

One of the fundamentals of this book is to let you know that if you want the fear and anxiety of public speaking to be completely eliminated, eradicated and extinguished from your life; the only way is to PRACTICE, PRACTICE, PRACTICE.

No amount of books you read (including mine) can replace practice. Books teach you methods and techniques. A book can work on changing your mind-set towards a given subject and can guide you into a reality that can motivate you to start practicing. However, if you do not practice, it is highly unlikely that you will ever conquer the fear and become a master of this skill.

Many people think the ability to speak publically will just fall on them like rain! For an exceptional few, yes, maybe, but for the majority of us, you need to learn it.

Public speaking is a skill, like driving. It can be learnt!

So, welcome to "70 Public Speaking Tips", where you will discover numerous methods, teachings, techniques and opportunities to practice the art of Public Speaking, and thereby reap all the benefits and advantages it can bring you!

Your public awaits…!

Enjoy

"I will pay more for a person who has good public speaking abilities" - Warren Buffet

Chapter One: Why You Need This Skill

As I alluded to in the introduction, public speaking is a skill, and because of that, anyone who is determined and willing can acquire it. Just as driving is a skill that anyone can get, so is public speaking. To consider that not anyone can speak publically is to say not everyone can drive. In reality, we know that anyone can drive, even if they have to take their tests 7, 10 or even 20 times and never give up. The reason you don't see many people driving is that if they fail to pass the test once or twice, most people give up.

My wife saw no reason to go on for yet another test after failing twice. But when we moved to an area where everyone needed to be mobile; she was so determined that she passed on the fifth attempt.

What most people do is that if they have a bad experience in public speaking, they stop doing it. The longer they leave it, the more they are reluctant to attempt it further, and it goes on like that until many live in constant fear. I have seen even people of colour go red when they are called to speak publically. Many would plead and beg not to be called to speak, even to a small audience.

But according to Warren Buffet, he will pay more to people who have good public speaking skills!

I want to give 3 reasons why you must be determined to acquire this skill.

#Tip 1
It creates the opportunity to impart others. Most people I have met have one heart cry, and that is the desire to impart others with what they know. While you are able to do this one-to-one, you can also do this one-to-many. If you are a great public speaker, you can impart many people at the same time. Either through a workshop, or seminar, or an event.

If you are not willing to learn this skill, your reach in life will be limited. Who wants to die with any regrets? Think about this—no matter how old you are now, project to the time you will be going to meet your Maker; who wants to know they could have impacted 1000 people, yet they only impacted 10 people because they did not learn a skill?

You are too important, plus, you know too much, and people need to hear from you. The sad truth is that people who are not as knowledgeable as you are, or possess less intellectual capabilities, are reaching people with their mediocre message, but you are still hugging your seat.

It is time for you to let your light shine and start delivering what you know to people who need to hear from you one-to-one, or in small or large groups!

#Tip 2

It creates more job and business opportunities. It will amaze you how many people have passed on great opportunities just because they knew it would involve some kind of public speaking. Sadly, what those people do not realise is that public speaking is one of the most fun, most rewarding, most personally satisfying activities you can ever be engaged in.

Did you know that the higher up the echelon of success you are, the more likely you will give presentations. This may be in the boardroom or large events.

If you avoid public speaking, you are basically single-headedly sabotaging your own career!

I even read at some point that people did not attend job interviews, even though they needed a job; just because they hated public speaking!

When it comes to public speaking, many lose sleep over their natural voice or accent. You will be understood if you deliver content that is relevant, from your heart, and meet the needs of people confidently and at a good pace.

Those who can communicate publically have a better selection of choices when it comes to careers and other opportunities. You can do it, too. You can learn and be better at public speaking.

#Tip 3
It creates the opportunity for increased revenue. Apart from the job prospects we discussed above, and their related salaries and responsibilities, there are other opportunities open to someone who can speak on any subject confidently.

It is not uncommon for well-known speakers to earn in excess of $50,000 a day to speak publically. According to Les Brown, he earned nearly $500,000 for a one day speaking engagement!

Some of these opportunities are:

- Running your own seminars
- Speaking as a guest at someone's seminar
- Guest speaking at an event
- Being on a panel with other speakers
- Video interviews

I hope I have managed to persuade you of the need to learn this vital skill. As we proceed further into the book, I want you to be determined that you will put into practice what you learn!

Action Point.
Be determined to practice what you learn from this book!

Buy This Book On Amazon

The Bad Girls Of The Bible - *7 Most Infamous*

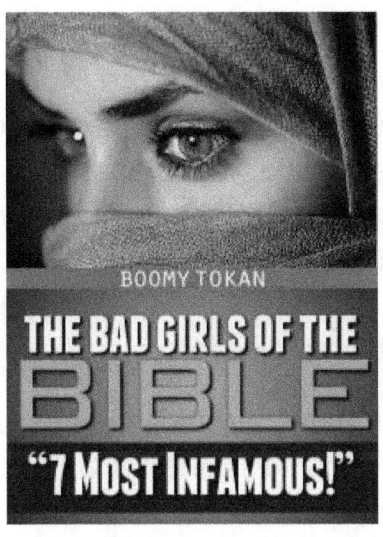

Ever wondered why some people are just – bad? In this book you will discover some well-known characters and other obscure ones that can teach you life lessons for the 21st Century. This book will educate and inspire you!

Read Introduction & Chapter 1
Bad Girls - Introduction

As I was driving to church one Sunday morning with the family, trying to arrive as early as we could, we were caught behind yet another set of traffic lights. I decided to take my mind off the hassle of traffic and focus on other things.

Suddenly, I started wondering about some of the most brutal women in the Bible. Since I love Bible quizzes I asked my wife to name some. There were the obvious ones of course, like Jezebel, but then the not so obvious characters like Athaliah, Micah's mother, who did more evil than even some of the most infamous biblical characters.

I began to think of penning this information into a book. This has taken a while, but here is the result. My aim is that you learn the lessons taught by the HOLY SPIRIT as you read through this book.

I also want you to remember two passages of the Bible.

We are told in 1 Corinthians 10:11, "**These things happened to them as examples and were written down as warnings for us, on whom the fulfilment of the ages has come.**"

And in **2 Timothy 2:15** the Bible says," **Do your best to present yourself to God as**

one approved, a workman who does not need to be ashamed and who correctly handles the word of truth."

I pray that this book will prepare you for a glorious future in CHRIST JESUS.

Remain blessed!

Enjoy!

Chapter One: Athaliah

Who is Athaliah?

Athaliah stood in a class all alone as one of the most vicious, cold-hearted killers in the Bible. Her actions had no bounds regarding age as she ravaged the kingdom in her effort to obliterate GOD'S will and establish her own!

Let's pick up the story about her in 2 Kings 8:26 which says:

Ahaziah was twenty-two years old when he became king, and he reigned in Jerusalem one year. His mother's name was Athaliah, a granddaughter of Omri king of Israel, So Jehoram marries Athaliah (house of Omri who was Ahab's father).They conceive a son called

Ahaziah, so Athaliah automatically becomes the Queen.

Let us look further at the origin of the whole family and the wickedness of Omri and Ahab. Omri came to power by assassinating the ruling king and in an effort to consolidate the strength of the nation; Ahab married Jezebel, the daughter of Ethbaal, who was King of the Sidonians. This relationship between Ahab and Jezebel produced Athaliah.

This is how the Bible describes Omri in 1 Kings 16:25-26:

^{25} But Omri did evil in the eyes of the Lord and sinned more than all those before him.^{26} He walked in all the ways of Jeroboam son of Nebat and in his sin, which he had caused Israel to commit, so that they provoked the Lord, the God of Israel, to anger by their worthless idols.

This is how the Bible describes Ahab in 1 Kings 16:30-33:

^{30} Ahab son of Omri did more evil in the eyes of the Lord than any of those before him.^{31} He not only considered it trivial to commit the sins of Jeroboam son of Nebat, but he also married Jezebel daughter of Ethbaal king of the

Sidonians, and began to serve Baal and worship him.³² He set up an altar for Baal in the temple of Baal that he built in Samaria.³³ Ahab also made an Asherah pole and did more to provoke the Lord, the God of Israel, to anger than all the kings of Israel before him.

This is how the Bible describes her own husband Jehoram in 2 Chronicles 22:13:

¹³ But you have walked in the ways of the kings of Israel, and you have led Judah and the people of Jerusalem to prostitute themselves, just as the house of Ahab did. You have also murdered your own brothers, members of your father's house, men who were better than you.

As we read about the household in which Athaliah was born, along with the marriage she had with Jehoram, it was almost expected that she would become evil; the only surprise was why she waited so long to show who she really was!

What did Athaliah do to make her one of the most infamous?

1. **She planned the destruction of GOD's ruling family.** *When Athaliah the mother of*

Ahaziah saw that her son was dead, she proceeded to destroy the whole royal family of the house of Judah. **2 Chronicles 22:10**

This action ranks as one of the most offensive and audacious. The Bible does not tell us the number of people she actually murdered, but it could have been as many as 300 people who could qualify for kingship when we reference back to the lineage of the male relatives of David.

The consequences of her actions could have impacted the coming of the Messiah. How? JESUS had to come from the family line of David, and if Athaliah had succeeded, there would have been no Jesus! In effect, her actions were perceivable just as evil as Herod's who orchestrated the killing of many children below the age of two in an effort to kill the Saviour, JESUS CHRIST.

2. **She taught her son to be evil.** *He too walked in the ways of the house of Ahab, for his mother encouraged him in doing wrong. ⁴ He did evil in the eyes of the Lord, as the house of Ahab had done, for after his father's death they became his advisers, to his undoing.* **2 Chronicles 22:3**

Mothers have a significant amount of influence in a child's life and their input has been known to shape the thoughts of a person as they grow. Therefore, a mother like Athaliah not only acted with evil intentions but encouraged her own son to propagate these evil actions as well. In those days we can infer that he murdered, stole, imprisoned, worshiped Baal, was involved in orgies and did nearly everything else imaginable that was evil.

3. **She took over the rule of Judah.** *He remained hidden with them at the temple of God for six years while Athaliah ruled the land.* **2 Chronicles 22:10**

Athaliah ruled by force. She showed no regard for GOD'S order or commands. She stood as the only female to become a king in Judah; she achieved this by murder and evil practice.

Her mind was so corrupt with evil that she even accused Jehoiada, the priest who was doing the right thing by installing Joash to the rulership of the nation, of committing treason! This comes from a woman who was a cold hearted murderer.

4. **She caused unrest for everyone in the nation.** *"...and all the people of the land*

rejoiced. And the city was quiet, because Athaliah had been slain with the sword." **2 Chronicles 23:21** We can tell the kind of state the people were living in at that time; it must have been governed by fear, established by force and delivered by the most corrupt type of people. We should note that Athaliah did not achieve her murderous status by herself; she must have persuaded others to join forces with her. We know this because of Jehoida's statement in **2 Chronicles 23:14**:

Jehoiada the priest sent out the commanders of units of a hundred, who were in charge of the troops, and said to them: "Bring her out between the ranks[b] and put to the sword anyone who follows her.

What can we in the 21st Century learn from Athaliah?

1. **Athaliah is definitely an example of how one's family environment can shape your future.** It is a fact that Athaliah came from an evil family and this biased her towards that direction; but she had a choice. Just because our background was of a particular kind does not mean that must be our future. We have seen people from broken families go on to have successful marriages. Life has to be

about going down a path we choose irrelevant of the previous environment we grew up in.

2. **One of the most alarming aspects of the events surrounding Athaliah's life is the length she went to achieve her ambition.** We need to watch ourselves and never get carried away because of what we want. In fact, our desires must be tempered with helping others and giving back to the community if we are to leave a good legacy.

3. **Walking in the fear of God.** Proverbs 9:10 and Psalm 111:10 say that "The fear of the LORD is the beginning of wisdom."Athaliah had no fear or regard for GOD or His people. Once that fear was absent, she could have taken almost any detestable action. We must always be governed by love for GOD and neighbours to prevent us from going astray and ensure we live a fulfilled life that impacts others in positive ways.

4. **Athaliah lived by the sword and died by the sword.** According to the law of sowing and reaping, Athaliah reaped what she had sown. She was a murderer who was also killed. James the Elder, in his letter in **James 3:12**, says, *My brothers, can a fig tree bear olives, or*

a grapevine bear figs? Neither can a salt spring produce fresh water.

We can derive from this that positive actions will result in positive results in our lives; what you choose to do will bear fruits for you!

5. **Athaliah caused unrest and people were happy when she was removed.** Anyone who is in leadership, either in the home, office, or business must have an attitude that JESUS had. He said in **Mark 10:45,** *"I did not come to be served but to serve and to give my life as a ransom to many."* If we do not live this way, people will rejoice when we are removed and that will be of no joy to us!

6. **Like Athaliah found out the hard way, God's sovereign plan can never be thwarted.** Job said this in **Job 42:2,** *"I know that you can do all things; no plan of yours can be thwarted."* This makes GOD sovereign. Rather than try to go against GOD'S plan, which is a fruitless effort, twenty-first century people should seek to know GOD'S plan and follow it!

Profile

Boomy Tokan is the founder and business tutor of **"Start Your Business in 30 Days" programme.** His experience spans across practical involvement in business and training of more than 1000 Start Up Business owners.

He has set up and run businesses in Property, Music, Management, and Fashion industries. **Many were very successful and others failed miserably.** Through them all he has learnt tremendous lessons that make him a knowledgeable, instructive and experienced teacher!

Whilst at Portobello Business Centre in London (One of the leading Enterprise Centres in Europe), **Boomy Tokan created and delivered Business** Training Programs plus One to One advice to Start Up Advice sessions.

He has also taught "The Business Planning" programme at City University London.

Over the past years **he has helped raise more than £300,000 (nearly $500,000) in small amounts for small businesses.** His experience on writing business plans and his understanding of how to raise finance has been of great benefit for many people.

As a Business Seminar Speaker he continues to contribute to the lives of many people.

Those who attend his courses say: "This facilitator knows what he is about and has a wide field of experience" Charles A

"I realise that I can just get up and do it…." Ros S

"Very insightful and encouraging" Precious O
"Great workshop" Peter D

"This workshop was very helpful" Lillian J and many more!

Boomy believes in giving back to the community and so he runs courses for Newham Business Start Up in London where he helps the underprivileged to access life transforming business information.

He has written over 100 articles for ezine.com and is a author of several books ("How to Write Your First Business Plan: With Outline and Templates Book"; "New Year's Resolutions: The Guide to Getting It Right"; "How to Raise Money for Your Business: The Ultimate Guide For Start Up

Businesses") published on Amazon Kindle that have entered the top 100 of the Entrepreneurship and motivational categories. His books are simply loaded with useful information that is life changing.

His book on **"How To Write Your First Business Plan" has received over Forty Two 5 Star reviews** with comments

like:

" This is really a comprehensive guide to writing a business plan." **Sandra**

" The book reads very easily, and the examples provided allow for a quick understanding of what the author is writing about." **Luke Glasscock**

" It was detailed while still maintaining a comprehensible overview of the structure and what should be taken into account when writing your business plan. " **Michael Matthews**

Have You Got Your FREE "Start Your Own Business In 30 Days" Guide

www.ingramcontent.com/pod-product-compliance
Lightning Source LLC
Chambersburg PA
CBHW051543170526
45165CB00002B/865